Tongue Screw

Cover design by Liz Kay

Book design by Liz Kay and Jen Lambert

ISBN: 978-0-9897837-4-3

Published by Spark Wheel Press

Tongue Screw

Heather Derr-Smith

Spark Wheel Press
Omaha, NE

Contents

"Perhaps everything that frightens us is,
in its deepest essence, something helpless that wants our love."
—Rilke, *Letters to a Young Poet*

Heathens

The hunters drove through town doing eighty,
the bodies of wolves tied in cruciform
to the hoods of their trucks.

The Pink Lady Slippers in the woods
hung like carcasses on hooks and the lights of ranches
twinkled in the valley below. We could hear,
with a kind of clairaudience, the stars clicking their pistols.

I stood at the edge of the world, tongue screwed shut.
But words came from all four corners—
even speechless, that power was unstoppable.

A red fox, like a blood smear
in the wild lilac of my mother's abandoned homestead,
and black-blotch shadows of hawks and ravens,
                              sweeping rorschachs—

The bird-like leaps of the heart's wonder.

My Stepfather Driving Away in his Trans Am

You shone, all metal and obsidian, fast down the driveway,
missing the heartbeat
of my heart skipping again with its grief.
I go down to the cow camp searching
for more lost pieces of you. A lure,
strung on an old fishing line. I recognize its jig and eye,

the one from the time we sat together by the pond, jack-light lit,
cicada's iterance of summer.
Fastening the hasps on the tackle box,
and night's cool breath was on my neck.
The season was about to turn,
a month later you're gunning the engine again, gone.

Advent

Birds pulse above the blood-black line of horizon.
I walk out through the sliding glass door into the backyard,

hoarfrost on the fallen leaves like thrush on a baby's tongue.

Over the chain link fence, three bald eagles fight for their kill
on the train tracks. My brother writes a postcard

from someplace near Bagram, fog veiling and unveiling
the Hindu Kush. In a dream he lifts his arm to cover his eyes

and I kiss the top-stitch scars along his mended wound.

In the middle of the night, a child screams awake.
But it's only the engine of the refrigerator, faintly.

The neighbor is a mystery, a stranger to us. He lives alone,
blinds shut at all times. I suspect what we all suspect.

Sometimes I stand in the dark of my window, facing the dark of his.

The Giraffe

Oranges, fallen from the trees, polka dot the lawn,
the smell so thick and astringent it stings my lips.

My father shows me the pomegranate vine clinging
to the chain link fence behind the Get-n-Go.

He's back in my life again, a trick. He comes
and goes, sometimes vanishing altogether

like a giraffe in the Roman Coliseum,
impossible to forget. In the aftermath of my awe, the breeze

with its blossomed scent zig-zags in the lace curtains,
swollen like pregnant bellies. Out the window,

high above the rooftops, is a V of migrating
American pelicans, snowy white with black-tipped wings,

how they float and hover like a song from a long time ago.
I just wait a few years longer and he reappears,

no idea how, sleight of hand, sudden,
as substantial as everything living, everything in its place.

Wilson's Promenade, Sarajevo, and Leonard Cohen

June and the lime trees were in bloom again.
Sontag said, *The century began in Sarajevo*
and it ended in Sarajevo.

A Leonard Cohen song in Bosnian
was tattooed on a girl's boney hip.
...her lover for a history-full of poems

Down in the bracken
I found a rabbit faking its own death, stark still
in a crown of thorns, in the shadow of the blooming limes.
These trees survived the war. Every war.
No one would cut them down.

The rabbit started hard, unblinking—
eye like a black stone,
until I reached out to touch it,
to put my whole hand in its side,
some proof of its life,

                          and it sprang
flash and nerve,
a blur of Lazarus bandages unraveling,

Our hearts all galloping resurrection hooves.

Tracking

The sutures of the dead wolf's skull,
were like outlines of the continents on a map of the world.

Half decomposed, he was once Alpha,
his remaining fur still speckled with ticks.

When he hunted, radiance exhaled from his mouth
like waters breaking from a new mother's legs.

A trail of blood led us to him,
his claws still extended with lash

and eschatology — *the part of theology concerned with death, judgment, and the final destiny of the soul and of humankind*
coming to find us out, revealed and known.

We are witnesses,

breaking and entering the infinite,
and what we find is no end to our loneliness.

Backfire

> The city's hieroglyphics
> appear from the haze as if
> we are descending

in a plane and hover right above the moment when words
become legible.

The air, like rough, white parchment,

> the chaparral in the Santa Monica Mountains continues to erupt

its desires, bush to bush beating their flashing hearts—

Helicopters fly low over the China graffiti and explosions of
bougainvillea.

We ascend the mountain's altar-stair to the Hollywood sign,

> glowing apparitional
> on the hill.

The diminutive orange trumpets of the sage blossoms blow

their small notes of color and scent.

> I want to be your young wife
thirty hours pregnant,

> Neruda opened at my pelvis.

> The lights of L.A. flicker
and reflex

like millions of votives in the temple. And I say it with Sappho,
Let it happen to me, all.

a writer of poems (a term usually reserved for writers of good poetry) like Pablo Nerud

16

The ravens, like hustlers, ascend the avocado tree.

a charred squirrel, insides spilled and lit up like black pearls—

When you rise to go
I'll turn into the cat-claw acacia,

                                        I'll hook your clothes. I'll hook a rib.
I was like the melanophila beetle

            who senses the fire from miles away

            and comes to lay her eggs in the heat.

A snake darts fast between us,

            dangerous as the look on my face, the look on yours.

Penuel

The wind rushes down the mountain of cellphone towers over
Los Angeles, ripping the slender pods of the oleander from its branches.

My heart's nargileh box swings on its chain,
embers glowing like the core of a volcano. (His body was beautiful,

swan wings, all force and flight and my bow was pulled back, taut with
aim.)

The fan hums and the blinds click.
Flames unhatch thousands of seeds, whispering bells and bishop pines.
Between us in that bedroom was the latching and unlatching of locks.

Somewhere near us a child's blood fills a vial.
A father's chest heaves. The world goes on,
its terrors assembling like an army.

The mule deer comes down from the fire, back covered in ash.

We remember something forgotten,
how the larkspur brushed our legs
on the day we first met,
how the California quail bust their sky blue breasts.

Like Jacob, I won't let go unless you bless me.

Tremble

The seals rose up out of the sea, breaking the radiant surface
of the Pacific and each creature seemed so solid
and strong, one would carry me,
steadying the sway of the world in the grasp of my hands.
Berryman said, the sea yearns, we ourselves flash and yearn.

I wanted so much, I shook, broke apart the bulwarks.

We wandered under the Santa Monica pier
and the waves were crashing up to my mouth,
filling me with salt. I was a pillar of desire.
As if I could be the one
worth a second look back.

There was a recording of gulls screaming
to scare away the pigeons. You parted my lips
and a dozen flew out.

Here, pry open this chest:
for you I would give
the juncos with their bellies full of mistletoe
and the long-legged bat, three embryos curled in her womb.

The San Gabriels rise up, fire out-flashing our longing for everything,
everything in this world we want and ache and hunger for and cannot hold,
like God undressing before Mary.

If Joseph had seen it, he'd have cut off his hands.

Crash

Once in your life you will desire something so forbidden
you will never recover from the shame, and at any moment

on a beautiful, clear day your skin will pull off like a glove
in an explosion, and down in the waters of the sea

right off the coast, under the airplane, kelp called laminaria
wave their striped blades, luminous under the navigation lights,

and here your metacarpals will drop out and be tossed by the currents
and wash up on the beaches of another world.

Look, the halophilia grass fades to the color of January
between your legs. Until then everything you ever desired

is what you have now. Paint the liverwort on the rocks.
Lead the mule deer to the mulberry tree. Hurry,

because in the twinkling of an eye,
God comes walking, swinging his purse of broken teeth.

Abduction

I don't know who kidnapped who. Your breath

like my own breath behind my burlap sack,
hand clenched around my wrist. We were bound

in this place, tottering and about to collapse.

It used to be an ocean here, the land covered in the Devonian sea,
 Nurse sharks nesting in the watery meadows underneath.

Marine birds migrate on the tide's anamnesis, expert hydrographers. And
your face was buried in my floating hair

like a small boy who barely escaped. You joined the resistance,
planted bombs in women's Jacuzzis and behind the melodeons.

I saw you in the club. Blood smeared on your face when you sang.
You have a creepy subtext, I said, just like me. Two gunmen in our masks.

The coyote trots down the middle of the suburban street

and a rabbit was caught and skinned on the barbed wire again.
But bless us. Our violent desire. Our violent want.
And bless, swooping over our heads and out of the dark, bless

the nightjars,
 folding their wings over the bracken of our grieving hearts.

I just wanted to belong to you, weave your veins through the loom
of my bones. Bless the tree, lightning-seared and charred.
Bless the upturned grave, mapped with reindeer lichen.

Bless our scars.

Raymond Fault, Los Angeles

Last night, the night-blooming thorn apple opened,
its white nightgowns strewn
along the edge of the road,
          and hundreds of moths skipped from silk to silk.

We were tripping on mushrooms and I could smell my mother's perfume,
trigger-warnings around every corner, the danger of our ordinary lives.

We stood on a precipice, overlooking the city, its lights dazzling
beneath the thick air of a storm and its dark arts coming in
over the threshold of the sea.

Thunder like gunplay in the canyon; lightning flashes
the chaparral and chamise, the flare in its bones ready to spark.
         Shrubs
If I had one of those scrolls,
                 I'd put it in my mouth.

In the morning the news said a human head had been found,
right along the road we had walked.

Twelve hours ago, estimated time of death,
the features of the face, they said, still fresh.

There's Mild Sexual Content, But Nothing Even Close to Sin

A house at the end of the woods
and a room with baby blue carpet.
A hope chest made of cedar
carved with the little girl's initials.

Her father stands in the doorway,
open to the approaching storm.
Bats flit, black hatchets slicing the air.

She begged him to protect her.
She pulled the mattress over her small frame,
earwigs dropping from the sheets.

The windows pop:
a vacuum like the look on his face when he left.

The waters above are held back from the waters below
said the Bible. Promise?

Do you remember when we were twelve once
and we met in a ditch,
knowing it was dangerous,
the smell of Noxema in the creek.

My stepfather said I had a tight little ass as I ran out the door.
Small leaves scattered on the sidewalk, like chips of nail polish, hot pink.

Somewhere the funnel rises
like a girl, mouth bound with cloth.

Butcher, Sarajevo

The chill air smelled of meat.
I wore a yellow belted dress and high heels the color of bologna.

You pressed your hip against me.
The hot afternoon waved in the windows.

The man behind the counter smiled,
two lovers in a foreign land.

Smoked pig trotters hung from the ceiling,
dangling their red painted toes.

Judith of Holofernes on Assignment in the Heartland

The bed is crowded with heartbeats,
adrenaline's frayed blankets up to the neck.
It's like this all night, some nights.

The sky relaxes its throat at sunrise.
Sweet-heart? Sweet-heart? calls the bird.
The sound of a blade sharpening, or a broken swing
hanging on its one hook.

Between the birth-stained mattresses, hid
a Damascene blade, crooked
as his cock,
using his own weapons against him.
If you're looking for violence
the song says you can always find it in a girl.

Does this make me just like my enemy?
If I had a photographic opportunity with a dozen of you naked,
would I light my cigarette and point and say click?

I see you under the collapsing pergola,
weighed down by concord grapes.
You fire up the grill. Hot coals glow.
In the backyard the Burlington roars,
sparks the dark along the railroad tracks,
shakes the house like a second coming.

Sun goes down in the yard
under a sidereal dome of sky.
Cherries and plums drop.
Did you ever sort of forget you're you?

Which one of us is it?
Now you swing by your own hair in my fist.

Family Dinner

Someone's opened up a doorway to the Occult,
my mother said. She can tell by the presence

in the house. My step-dad started drinking again,
can't take his eyes off my breasts. Tobacco smoke

curls into the humid night, as he sits smoking
in the screened-in porch, black-light zapping the bugs.

I imagine he is wonderful to me, call him *Daddy*
like a Southern girl does. I learn to cook,

wanting to please him, hoping the ruffle of my apron
will catch his eye. The cicadas whirr

and the owls turn their heads to watch. My step-dad
drags on his cigarette and the ember glows

like a popped hymen, with its flash of pain and light
in the dark where the girl lays, having crossed over

to some promise land of love. He smells of Old Spice.

He says, you are just like your mother, so controlling.
He throws the peach cobbler in the sink, shouts

Why can't you cook something someone wants to eat?
My mom snaps her fingers and says, if you aren't sure

you're saved then maybe you aren't really saved.
My brother says he would never marry any girl

who wasn't a virgin. My mom says, shhh you'll hurt
your sister's feelings.

Interrogation I

I've given up on him. You can't get anything
out of that heart with honey. I could not
sleep all night. It felt like there was a spring
between my legs, bees in my chest. I half-dreamt
of a row of hapless cars caught in a storm,
a hurricane that blew down the Eucalyptus,
and uprooted even the cacti and the chain link.
All chaos broke loose and the small anoles
were singing Guantanamera down at the old
Square of the Weapons. It was a bad dream.
I was glad to get out of there. It's like that with him.
He reminds me of someone I know. I walk through
the rain shadow, dust as dry as the truth,
nothing much to it. Listen: dusk's hymnary opens
and songs fall out of the mangrove's cool, dark
mouth. Give me the camera and the hammer
and what he's most afraid of, and I'll make him sing.

The Schools of Fish We Catch at Night by the Light of Powerful Lamps, Istanbul

Under the magenta blossoms of Judas trees, I think of you.
Red and white cylinders hang like lit candles.

They say it is painfully beautiful in April and May.
God made spring for us as a test. I barely got through customs.

Shoals of tunny swam in the waters of the Marmara.
The people made ships from the wood of demolished houses
                           and the braided ropes of women's hair.

                 I'm no longer a pacifist.

I step out on the back of the sea and the waves carry me,
                 the water's bandages lapping at my hands.

We file through the airport security, clutching our shoes,
our bodies lit up in the scanner's back-scatter,

a million points of light like virgin lamps burning.
I'm not afraid of war anymore.

Incarnation

Wind blows around your body and there you are
    beside the cairn, its stacks
of field stones weathered down smooth by storms
    and fires. The new grass is breaking you to

small pieces. Vast flocks of lapwings swayed
    from side to side like some drunk stumbling
through the sunlight. We were both baptised
    and demonic. Andy Goldsworthy says we often forget

that we are nature. Hitch and hiccup of wrens

and I'm down on my knees again giving a stranger
    a blow job. Butcher birds in the hedgerow,
the storm coming over the ridge like a buzz saw in the trees.
    I wanted to be connected, like seeing God

and remaining alive after seeing him. You promised
to stitch me new clothes. Alone in this garden,
the wind holds us, the saw grass lisps.
    On the cusp of some unnamed flower, the wasp.

Energumen

Walnuts in their secret planets drop on the ground all around us.
Hundreds of purple mallow rhyme across the fields.

Take the aril of my tongue and stitch it to the earth.
Bloom my dark fruit from pawpaw flower.

I'm the girl with the scythe in the song of the lark.
I'm the heart still throbbing in the dead horse.

My hands irrupt into the limbs
of the spindle tree, its autumn blaze,

my oily bones sequined with drops of rain.

Every direction I walk
I evoke this power within me.

Follow the coyote's tracks in the arroyo
                to this one moment, hovering in the dark above you

Grind, you say, *Now, grind*

Interrogation II

We have gotten to know one another so well. I could
capture you and recapture you. The fretwork
of your bones, your flesh like water beneath my palms.
Here I am and there you are, and memory beats the door
between us, an illuminated text on your lips, and in the morning
the question remains, *who are you?* In a Ciglane apartment,
in an ordinary room, residue of gunpowder on your finger tips.
Above us, the fluorescent drop light swings on its cord.
My stepfather had one like that, did yours?
It swung in the basement over the spinning blades
of saws. Machines screaming, the smell of pine shavings,
cat urine, and cologne. He was a soldier. I hid from him.
Did you love your father? Your chest smells like sawdust.
I know so much about you and nothing at all.
You come straight out of my
basement like a bad dream, ready to explode. I run
through the labyrinth of your body and mine, where
does one country begin and the other end? Never mind,
there are checkpoints and dragon's teeth to keep things
in order. Where were you the morning after I spent
the night in Hamburg, nineteen and on ecstasy?
I might have loved you then, but you were just a thing,
a photograph of two men kissing. No, I forgot.
That was a different time and another place, raves
and all of us naked, staggering with love.
There was a war on here, disputed territory. You
were a refugee, much younger than me, curled
in your mother's lap, the smell of her, apples
and roses. Her mouth tasted like bitter almonds.
And here you are now, spitting image. I came to save you,
but then you saved me. I can't decide if we are brothers
in arms or enemies, freedom fighters or terrorists.
Where did you get that giant head? It looks like Goliath.
I would call that contraband. I think there will be
repercussions. I'll have to turn you in, again.

Impartation, Sarajevo, Bosnia

Wind Chill Warning. I pass a half-dozen wrecks,
a jack-knifed semi,

                  a sports car split in two,
driverless.

                Crossing the bridge, I look down
on the snowy white bend of the frozen River Miljacka.
50 below zero. Flocks of geese huddle,
a convocation of dark bodies on the ice.

                Steam rises from them, mists like feathers in ascent,
hundreds of ghosts unwrapped from their packages.

Rhododendron

1.

I had a summer job watering plants in a nursery
in the middle of nowhere. Some redneck county

lost between ribbons of blue highway. I wanted
that flower, the color of a shadow's dark sex,

a cardinal come to rest between my legs. I stole
the whole damn bush, stuffed it in the back seat,

its woody branches scraping the upholstery. Be careful,
my mother warned me that morning before I left,

there's some guy in the Food Lion parking lot
stuffs women in the trunk of his car. And on the same

highway I drove every day, another man
pulled up beside the truck of a Mennonite girl

and mouthed into the speeding wind:
Your tire is flat and she read his lips and believed.

2.

My mom said she could just feel the power
of darkness out there and no girl should be alone

in that country. Driving home one afternoon
I took a shortcut and got lost, the whole world

seemed to pivot and switch, directionless.
I stopped at an old general store for help

and a man led me behind a door to a small room
and told me to undress. It was too late.

There was nothing I could do.
Small frogs hymned faintly their evensong

from the throats of the pitcher plants.
He let me go, but a few weeks later

they found the Mennonite girl's body in a ditch.

Thrown, Sarajevo

I saw a house being carried down river.
It started in one place and ended in another.

Wild dogs, nipples black with new birth,
shuffle back at the edge of the wood.

From the bridge in view of the house, I threw
every gift you ever gave me: shawl

of pink rabbit fur, the complete works
of Sylvia Plath in Bosnian, a framed photograph

of my daughter and your daughter (hard to tell
who is who, except by instinct). The bridge

sways and trembles, flood waters too high,
current too strong. No Thru Traffic.

Orange cones warding us off. Ten years
after the war and still *Opasna Zona,*

Danger Zone, everywhere, impossible
to leave it behind. Heat lifts from the guts

of dead fish and the wreaths of trash
on the water's edge, flood still rising

about to burst its crest.

Tracers

In our Ottoman room in Old Sarajevo, after the fight,
I wash your hands, bloodied by shards of glass.

When you breathe in the dark I lay bewildered.

Here we are balanced on the knife's edge of past
and present. The call to prayer severs the hours,

dislocated like that, we fumble in the dark at our clothes.

A famous poet walks through the park
where the Bosnian lilies open their mouths
and the Bogomil dead are cradled under their tipping stones.

Let it be known, no travelers on earth, nor stars in the sky
can get lost in this place

Wood smoke pools in the valley of Sarajevo,
beneath the mountains. It spools in my hair—
you brush it out in wisps.

Here in this city is the scandal of the particular:

the tracers of bullets burning brightly in their trajectory
the scissors they used to cut off a child's underpants in the morgue
the eggs left coddling on the stove of someone

who has vanished

In the mountains is a fire over land not yet de-mined.
There is no way to extinguish it.
It must burn itself out.

Traitor

You were always so afraid. The loss you lived with
was too much. Maybe you were born with skin
that stung in the rain. Maybe the light hurt you
more than others. I sought you out, called gently
from my childhood self, like calling a cat home
from the dark woods, careful not to spook it,
hoping that you would come back to me,
come out of your dark, folded heart and just sit
beside me, reading a story I loved. But you stayed
hidden. Behind your open mouth, its teeth in the O
of anger, behind the shut lids of your eyes,
blistered by rage. The note from the woman you found
in your husband's pocket. The poem I wrote
about an old woman and you thought it was you,
it must be you, always you on some stake or rack—
because of course I had to be bad, something cold
born out of your womb, some ultimate betrayal. After all,
you did for me, nearly dying to birth me,
of course, I had to be a traitor. It was the only thing
you knew was real, the pain you felt, had to feel.

Runaways

1989 and we were homeless and seventeen. We slept on the rooftops
at the dusk and dawn edge of downtown and in the attic

of George Washington's boyhood home, a building abandoned
on the edge of the woods. Pigeons roosted on one end of our room

and cooed us to sleep and awake. The world in its indifferent beauty
went on, whether we were hungry or scared, its threads of cells
unraveling

and raveling again, like the ghost of my great grandmother in her
Mennonite kapp, knotting and unknotting a red string for healing fevers
or casting a hex.

You could hear the spade-foot toads and leopard frogs weaving their
songs in the pond, the rush of blood and pulse of fear, when the police
lights swooped

over the darkened catalpa tree below our window and washed
across the skin over the delicate ribs of your caged chest,

turning you blue like a corpse. We froze
like startled creatures and hid, waiting for danger to pass, alive with
terror.

You shot up and I held your body, slumped like a pietà. Forgive
the sentimental memory, forgive the nostalgia for near death, the trauma
bonds,

but we were human, our flesh gorgeous as the glitter and dazzle of
sunlight on water. We wanted to kill ourselves but not to die. You fell
asleep in my lap

and I didn't move all night so as not to wake you, your help-meet.
We wanted to protect one another. It was the best we knew how to love.

Men would come around to buy drugs and my body would become a lure
and spell, and I wanted it, to be like a stag,
                        wanted so much I staggered under lust's weight
                antlers top heavy with desire,
                                        shot through with arrows.

But you were headship, hedge of protection, You said,
you don't have to give yourself away, you don't have to do that—

and you warned me there would be nothing left. And then you fucked me
violently against the dirty floor. But you were wrong., what's left is all of it

and it's mine as well as yours. All the beauty and the terror, Rilke said.
There's more to this story than just us: Bats hung like plums in the branches

of evening light. Night herons flew at dusk silhouetted in the shape
of warplanes, against a sky glowing with particulates. Bitterns boomed their
throats

in the wetlands and the wastes, and you could hear them if you'd still a while
and barely breathe and listen. The eyelids of the redbud blossoms fluttered.

Between us white pelicans would float like angels, completely at ease in their
hover, unrolling the scrolls of their wings, as if they meant to tell us
the truth, a book of life written in their hollow bones,
                        leading us forward in the direction of home.

Please Report Any Suspicious Activity

A storm flashed outside the stained glass of the church,
hail knocking against the tin roof of the bell tower.

Lightning cleaved it right in half,
just like a story with a moral at the end.

The women of the town tended their gardens.
Surprise lilies burst from the ground like clockwork.

But down in the river, under the baptisms and tire swings,
lampreys sharpened their concentric rows of teeth.

The town's burnt spire and fall foliage and flea markets,
football lights flooding the playing fields and the moths

like burnt paper flutter through the air.

If you tell my secrets, she said to her ex, *I swear to God,
I will cut myself open from throat to crotch.*

The crowd cheers.

Hound of Love

That beagle wears my patience and my love, disobedient,
humping the stuffed gorilla.

Two girls fell asleep out on the creosote. Hard to believe,
                    but it happened right here, in this town,
                                    and the thing is,
                                            the girls survived.

The red-eyed vireos, beaks stained purple, drop elderberries to the ground.
Yellow jackets swarm over the pulp.

A picture my six year old made:
Dear Mom, and it's me in a boat being decapitated by a scythe.

I watched my oldest daughter lying on her bed beside her sleeping little sister.
The oldest caressed the naked arm of the youngest
and then reached out to smooth her hair.

She thought they were alone.
She did not see me, watching from behind the cracked door.

I was surprised that she could love her
without knowing I was there.

The dog catches the scent, pulling against the leash

to get to the place where we gathered, our own Gethsemane,
waiting half the night for someone to show,

just a stone's throw. We lead the witnesses to the spot
still stained with blood.

Megas Phones, Sarajevo

The sky is expanse. God did not say
let there be anything. He just said.

A man on a bike flashes by the bay window. The Miljacka stinks.
The cat catches the bee at the garden door,
beneath the call to prayer in the backyard of the Ottoman apartment.

If you look up, you can see the bullhorn of the mosque
on its telephone-pole tower, a voice

calls and calls to our rising and falling.

Yellow butterflies bounce over the asphalt.
A goldfinch bends its head to pass under the Linden tree.
The tiny egg-shaped fungi of the birds-nest-mushroom leap in the rain.

Darwin said, endless forms most beautiful and most wonderful.

The grass slits the thousands
of dark soiled wrists in the Martyr's cemetery.
The birds do their sobbing behind the blue curtains.

Flocks of birds come from the mountains in every direction,
jealous as angels of us, peering into our rooms.

God sleeps with teenagers. The power lines hum
and the trams clatter past the old JNA barracks, still blackened with soot.

He's unchanging from Beginning to End.

Time has worn its chest out is the word for seduction
in some ancient Arabic poem.
I gave him his head without reins, is another translation.

My daughter says, *Gloria Dei,* and asks what it means.

At the Old Jewish Cemetery, Sarajevo, with Tom Violence and the Sparrow

We found a curled snail
in the burial hole
sucking with its mouth
at the salty stones

We stood dumbstruck
at the lip of the bullet-pocked grave
I thought of the saint

whose cut head kept singing

Holding on for dear life
My tongue is tied
I know he watches me

How beautiful
was your naked chest
carved with a knife
your singing head,
your rising bliss

How beautiful,
the sparrow's nest
mended with spider silk

On Mt. Trebevic, mists drag and tatter
in the maidenhair ferns

The cuneiform
of a Linden leaf
The seams of grasses
The boys kissing
beside the pregnant
mounds of dirt

Sing any song, sing every song.
Rilke said praise is all that matters.

Solstice, Sarajevo

The eel's black whips quiver.
In the bay window a passionflower vine climbs its trellis.

I never gave much thought to beginnings or endings.

The sky unfolds its parchment. Snow
like human dust dissolves into the river.

Fish dart in their glass-slipper shapes.

A man waits outside the window with the face of a white shell
curved inward and hundreds of sharp teeth.
He was once someone to me.

The water disorients with its darknesses overlapping.
The light you give off did not come from a pelvis, said Rumi.
In winter, here, light comes from the ground.

We hold our candles to our faces, look forward and look back,
the cast of light on the thin skin over her hyoid bone.

We remember summer's purple lupine, big as human thighs.

Gnats

Delphinium sways in the warm Shenandoah air,
humid with a storm coming in. Thunder drums

in the county over. The leaves upturn their bellies
and silver flash. The lambs start their bleat

from the Mennonite farm next door.
I can't get rid of you, ghost, Mother

banging on the door. Your harm
over my head, threatening to descend

into my breath and shut it. The lambs
are frantic now, the clouds hemorrhaging

with blue tongues.

When I was a child I begged from you,
there in the dirt, a hipbone

its cup-shaped pocket I longed to drink
from. You evaporated with the mist from the ground,

the tiny gnats of your love buzzing off.

Plymouth Fury, 1988-2015

Driving cross-country, the blue light just before dawn like a sea.

Catalpas loosen their morning throats
$\qquad\qquad\qquad\qquad$ knife-slit pink,
veins that lure the honeybee in—
a lack of modesty.

The hypodermic needle of you still shuddering beneath the night's skin.

$\qquad\qquad\qquad\qquad$ ***

I drive it all back behind me, drive it back toward the Atlantic, going west.

Speak low,

trying to forget, hold the arousal of your ghost under the water,
your head under the waves,
$\qquad\qquad\qquad\qquad$ foam in your hair like blown stars, like semen
$\qquad\qquad\qquad\qquad\qquad\qquad$ exploding between my legs.

$\qquad\qquad\qquad\qquad$ ***

$\qquad\qquad$ The windshield bursts with the bodies of mayflies

$\qquad\qquad$ wings stippling the glass, delicate capillaries and threads.

Wind gusts through the open window over my body,
$\qquad\qquad\qquad\qquad$ Patti Smith and Kim Gordon on the stereo,

cigarette ash scatters against the backseat,
dissolving like snowflakes on the blue vinyl,

sometimes burning like stigmata,

where we, when we were homeless, once slept, our bodies unflinching.

***

The view from where we parked, city below us,
Fredericksburg battlefields, Sunken Road, and Marye's Heights, its hilltop

levitating

on the horizon, soil still soaked in gore, built with bones.
Hundreds of years later

and it all remains,
in the scents of boxwood and loam and lichen and moss—
in the taste of the air—cold iron of the bricks from the cemetery wall.
Memory's sudden hold on you, a grasp and then a loosening,

like a man inside a woman's body, or a woman's fingers
                                        inside the body of a man.

You remember a past like the residue of gunpowder on your hands,
blood on your sleeve. The gravestones
of the Confederate dead and the Union dead glow in the dark
                                        and from this distance

seem to drift like puffs of smoke.

***

We hid in each other's
hips and in each other's sides,

where God pulled out ribs to make each other out of us.
That was our myth,
a bewilderment, a tie that binds.

                              We smashed in the windows
of the bar and pried open the cash register,
just enough money for rent.

We moved from the backseat of the car
to an apartment that smelled of vomit

                              where I crouched low in domestic prostration
with a bucket of soap to scrub the bloodstains from the floorboards,
                              and the water turned black from my sponge.

I reveled in it, house and keeping.

                              ***

There was a clawfoot tub in the bathroom in the hall and a window so dirty
it filtered the sun and hid us from view.
Your bones jutted
from your pelvis and shoulders
                         and I washed your body, seventeen,
still missing your mother
                         two years after she'd thrown you out. My hands
took the place of her (swear no harm)
and found you, shelter and small acreage.

            This was the home we made out of our homelessness.

                              ***

We did whippits and Jagermeister shots until we turned blue
and lost our voice. All that speechless excess.

Downstairs below us a child screamed when a man came into her room.
We could hear

her through the vent in the floor saying *no. no. no. no.*

***

    This dawn light is the same, again and again. It is blue.
    It repeats itself like a chorus *Shall not loveliness be loved forever?*

    It is vibrant and liquid. It is resurrection, waiting for you
    to come back to it, meet it at that replica moment, at the pivot
    and edge between last night and morning. It is radiant blue.
    It is the same exact light
            you can always return to.

***

The car hurtles under the arbor of oaks, the wreaths and crowns of
kudzu
        boughs of the trees bowing like prayers or praise—

And what do we praise? What hymns
what bell, what harp, do we pluck and prick?

Kim Gordon said, the word is *fuck.*

Praise us, our black eyes, our thin wrists, and dirty hair—
praise for our fumbling with buttons and zippers, praise me touching
myself and then touching you with that light,
            liquid from between my legs.

There was so little we knew. Praise us anyway. Praise the miscarriage
I bled and wrapped up in our only sheet.
All the life we desired and consumed, spitting it
      back out on each other's bodies.

    Praise the body. Your body. And mine.

***

Follow the road under the cathedral of trees,

twisting and climbing the mountains,

                    the hollows in their vaginal dark, the hounds
skirting the lip of the creek,
and the cliffs that seep springwater onto the asphalt.
                    Follow the road, the red-wing blackbirds
trilling on their tips of grass in the ditches,

the sky in its blue gown, clouds like white lilies

and the wind always opening its mouth, sucking at my hair, my hands
memory's blankets pulled back,

the porcelain clawfoot tub empty and drained and cold in its hard form,

no water to hold your scarred arms and your delicate neck.
You're gone one minute
and then you're back in the car again, back under my skin,
                              a star marking the map.

You once said *run* and I ran.

***

            I saw a photograph of you twenty years later
at the Whitney, famous now, a rockstar. (The car, I sold a long time ago.)

  In the photograph your head was bent, hiding your face behind your hair,

            but there was the form of you,

                    the grace and proof of you, untouchable

and impossible to erase—

In the photograph you stood

before a massive ink drawing that covered an entire wall,

      tangled web of lines like threads unspooled on the blank page—

and you were looking down, legs crossed,
      still wearing combat boots and skinny jeans,

—so that I cannot see your face, where surely the years would show
as they do on mine—

But I saw you in the flesh again as you were when we were so young,

      in that infallible light memory steps back into—*can* it be
      carnal and infallible at the same time? Transfigured

exactly as I once knew you, a trick of physics,
as if we could still be blameless,

undressing,

                the trace of you perfect in its frame.

Hundred Year Flood

I walked home with my young son
from the town's one movie house. All around us

the risen river lapped at the yards. It was dusk
and we could hear the waves and sense

the current's presence.

Dozens of hummingbirds buzzed around a bush.
It was the faintest of apparitions hastening in the dark.

My father taught me how to find their nests
in the trees of the Dollar store parking lot,

little purses of spun spider silk.

The red stalks of the fire-moss flamed in spring.
Every few years now there's a hundred year flood.

Back at home, locked in his room, my son
punched the electrical outlets,

cut his arms with the broken shards.

Look, we said together, the waters part,
like revelation's open door no one is able to shut.

Adonai

I cannot sing like they sing, in four part harmony,
those Mennonite songs,
        Sweet Hour of Prayer rubbing its tongue
all over the tiny hairs on the nape
        of my neck, motes of dust swirling
around the kerosene lamps, their voices
        against the drum of my ear like blood
spilling on the floor and seeping under the pews
        and down the shaft of my throat.
I want to mop it up with my blouse,
        swallow it down like semen into the earth
        and the tilled fields, *beat your swords into ploughshares*
        she says, her hand on the hilt. The song
              rises
back up to lick itself again, chords thrumming
        its milk and the night moths fluttering
around the new corn's silks.
        I want to sing with you here, worship with you,
say your name out loud, Stranger.
        Grief adjoining joy. I fall in love like this,
        swallows careening out of the bruised
bluffs of me, the cliffs of dusk, too much
for anyone to take. I'd slice myself open for you,
        the veal of the unborn calf set on the table of my
              abdomen,
the spider spinning her bobbin on the tulip's bodice
        against my sacrum, all the bodhisattvas of the forest
behind clavicle and sternum, my stomach.
Sick with love, love like a blue jay's dagger,
        body snatcher, this, the bloody mindedness
of how I love. It'll wear you down.
The air soaked with the hymn's soft rain thumbing
        in my uncovered hair. A song woven through
the heddles and reeds of a loom, looping
        around to its next verse and next,
until it hushes out and the heart goes deaf.

Snatch

You'll get no way out, no Ariadne for you.
I assembled a collection of blades
made from the shoots of arrow roots.

Write the end of your story:
He becomes top-heavy with antlers.
His own hounds bring him down.

I wrote the body as a charm and hex.
Carved a spell on my scapula.
Said, tell me the secret names of things.

My stepfather accused me of being just like my mother,
so controlling and he kicked me down the hall.
Mother burnt those spells
in the bathroom sink, Satanic,
the ink blood-let into ash, begged me to repent.

I sang the *Dies Irae* at the top of the stairs.
I pulled my hair out by the roots,
bits of flesh still glued to the shafts.

Home was a bad love,
the kind that gouges out your eyes
and leads you by the hand into the labyrinth.
The kind that promises to hold onto you forever.

I smashed the windows of that house,
broke the glass to smithereens
and fled into the woods called Wilderness,

the ghostly tracheas pushing up
from the old battlegrounds,
where the soldiers died, all split open and hemorrhaging

on the bruised magnolia blossoms in the dirt,
like the sloughed off vaginas of the dead.
I kissed between the legs of soldiers beside the roar
of the Rappahannock,
bodies cocked against the dogwood trees, petals in my hair.

I turned every curse back on that house.
                                What recourse did I have, but to open this book,
incant my fractured self into existence?

I took off my shirt,
nipples the color of bubblegum, offered myself up to the world
nympholeptic
like the Anabaptist woman, naked,

holding her two lopped off breasts in her hands,
still singing her hymn,
unwilling to recant.

Touch

I only wanted
to brush against
one place or two—
my breath
on the small bone
at your wrist
or a kiss
on a taste bud,
a lash, the lip
of a single hair
on your arm,
like a sepal,

antenna, so slight
I'd be nothing
but light.

I'd carve
a tiny abolitionist's
coat button

a miniature
daguerreotype
of two diminutive
folded hands
ringed in gold.

Scenes from

the Story of Joseph
carved in ivory,
on the handle
of a comb.

The Fall of Phaethon
in onyx
the size of a plum.

I would not intrude,
tiptoe in

like mice sniffing
the air,

each pad foot
the size of a pearl
that rolls away
beneath the bed.

If you wanted me,
I would turn
into a girl for you,
do anything, bow,
disappear.

Confession

A wagon of Mennonite girls passes by on the dirt road,
calico cape-dresses and Jacki-O sunglasses.

Adagio of trout in the stream,
abracadabra of wind in the willows over the water

and the sky like a battlefield,
the aerobatics and ballistics of birds.

All of it so beautiful,
like bones we might reassemble and redeem
from the damned,
quiver the vertebrae into place,
snap the atlas in its lock

and the world will rest in Sabbath, at last.

I wanted to be loved, shut up in the ark
like something worth saving, didn't *you?* Didn't *you?*

Blessed art thou
                    by whose word all things come into being.

Dove, Sarajevo

Wyeth said our art is only as strong as our love.
How even the most hateful or drunk loved
ferociously with their bayonets and collisions.
How they gnawed, thrust and stabbed,
dismembered love, and loved every piece,
loved the finger and toe and tongue of love.

I watch the children playing baseball
in the barren lot and see myself, a girl among them
in this forgotten city at the center of the world.
I swing my stick at the ball and leap
into the air, dust tornadoing my heels,
flash of fugue, darting
past the graffitied wall,
faster than my hyperventilated breath,
from imaginary base to base, Champion!

It's like that, hurtling into the future,
how I freight you with me
along the tracks going downtown,
the clickclick of my insistent pulse
following the arterial maze
into the stacked apartment complex of Ciglane
tongue-tied with murals and text, *Wordsdonotmean
anythingtodayThingsgotoutofcontrol*

mercenary and militia and martyr to love.
Below us, the Miljacka dazzling with lights
of mosque and minaret. Hold on, I won't let go of you,
your body tearing from your bones, like a flayed dove
dangling by a thread. It's still you, unspooled
out of my fist, explosion of feathers, skein of tissue,
I won't give up, foot pressed against the undetonated mine,
                                                          and lift.
It's still love, it's still love, it's still love.

May We Meet No Line a Boundary

Sometimes I return to my mother's childhood home, believing
I can reclaim it.

Mists rise off the frozen creek
and the red star of Betelgeuse blinks out.

Pools of snowmelt glitter
violet as the Wyoming iolite. This is her territory, not mine,
her mother's grave and her father's.

I track it, the old paths of a past life.
The martin's pad foot prints the mud,
claws curled into slivers of an unspoken language.

It's mine now. I've nearly caught up with it,
right at the hem of the garment.

The red wing blackbird pivots
and shifts on its tall switch.
At first bright re-ignition of morning light,
the snake hushes in the saltbush
and lifts its rattle to astonish us.

Notes

Rilke: *Letters to a Young Poet*

"Wilson's Promenade, Sarajevo, and Leonard Cohen": Stranger Music: Selected Poems and Songs, First Vinatge Books. 1993.

"Backfire": Sappho: A New Translation, University of California Press, 1958

"Tremble": "Dream Song 14" John Berryman

"There's Mild Sexual Content but Nothing Even Close to Sin": Job 12:15

"At the Old Jewish Cemetery, Tom Violence and the Sparrow": "Tom Violence" Sonic Youth, Evol; 1986

"His Eye is on the Sparrow" Civilla D. Martin; 1905

"Plymouth Fury": "Flower" Kim Gordon, Bad Moon Rising, 1985

"Snatch": Ovid's Metamorphoses

Acknowledgments

Many thanks to friends who have walked beside me in life and in poetry or who I met in the briefest of hours and was left with a spark and a trace: Todd Smith, Ray Nelson, Diane Gingerich-Feil, Amy Woolard, Chris Kasper, John Clark, Sean Walker, Jim Danger Coppoc, Dan Coffey, Jen McClung, Fielding Wilson, Velid Beganović, Stephen Watson and Ben Apatoff.

And special thanks to my editors and new poetry sisters, Liz Kay and Jen Lambert who joined their own hearts with mine in the making of this book.

"Heathen," "Rhododendron," and "Hundred Year Flood" published at *The Center for Mennonite Writing*, " The Giraffe" and "Family Dinner" published at *Rusty Toque*, "Butcher, Sarajevo" and "Wilson's Promenade" published at *2River View*, "Interrogation II" and parts of "Confession" published at *Diode*, "Megas Phones" published at *Tiferet*, "Hound of Love" published at *Weave*, "Advent" published at *Barn Owl Review*, "Field of Blackbirds" and "In the Old Jewish Cemetery with Tom Violence and the Sparrow" published at *Ruminate*, "The Schools of Fish we Caught at Night by the Light of Powerful Lamps" published at *Literary Bohemian*, "Backfire" and "Energumen" published at *Nashville Review*, "Thrown" published at *34th Parallel*, "Shelter "published at Off Channel, "Interrogation I" published at *Brink*, "Traitor" published at Ink Node, "Crash" and "Raymond Fault" published at *Natural Bridge* and "Impartation" published at *Valparaiso Review*.

About the Author

Heather Derr-Smith was born in Dallas, Texas in 1971. She spent most of her childhood in Fredericksburg, Virginia. She earned her B.A. in Art History from the University of Virginia, where she also took poetry workshops with Charles Wright, Rita Dove, and Greg Orr. She went on to earn her MFA from the Iowa Writers' Workshop and has published two books of poems, *Each End of the World* (Main Street Rag Press, 2005) and *The Bride Minaret* (University of Akron Press, 2008).

Printed in the USA
CPSIA information can be obtained
at www.ICGtesting.com
LVHW091931171123
764249LV00007B/1322